DISCOVER
Ancient
Treasures

By Cynthia Benjamin

Celebration Press
Pearson Learning Group

Contents

Looking For Clues

Have you ever looked at a piece of clothing, a book, or a photo album that has been in your family for many years? You might find such family treasures in your attic or garage. At first, they might not seem very important to you, but if you examine them more closely, you might think about the people who made them. Where and how did they live? What were their lives like?

Items such as an old embroidered shawl or old photo would be considered **artifacts** by **archaeologists**. These scientists study artifacts and other evidence that explains how people lived long ago. By discovering and learning about something owned by your family that was created many years ago, you would be doing what archaeologists do—and it could all start by cleaning out your attic!

You might discover treasures like these in your attic or garage.

3

In the science of **archaeology**, scientists learn about different cultures that existed in the past by studying clues these societies left behind. Just think of an archaeologist as a scientific detective. In addition to studying such artifacts as ancient pottery or tools, archaeologists also study the things that were lost or thrown away by ancient peoples. Archaeologists call this rubbish **midden**. Think about what you throw away every day. An archaeologist in the future could tell a lot about your daily life by examining your trash.

Archaeologists look for clues at sites on the ground or underwater. Underwater archaeology became easier as more advanced diving devices were developed, such as Aqualungs, which helped divers to breathe underwater. Another technological advance called **sonar scanning** uses sound waves to find underwater objects.

Whether researching land or underwater sites, most archaeologists follow a scientific method called the "archaeological search process." This process involves

◈ asking good research questions.
◈ doing background research.
◈ excavating the site.
◈ performing a laboratory analysis of artifacts.
◈ sharing findings in a published report.
◈ curating, or storing the materials and information.

Think about this method as you learn more about excavations in Egypt, the American Southwest, and Peru.

King Tut: The Boy King of Ancient Egypt

Tutankhamen's solid gold face mask, made in the 14th century B.C., is now on display in the Egyptian Museum in Cairo, Egypt.

Ancient Egyptian civilization first developed on the banks of the Nile River about 5,000 years ago. **Pharaohs** ruled ancient Egypt for thousands of years. Tutankhamen was only nine years old when he became Pharaoh. He ruled from about 1347 B.C. until his death about 1339 B.C.

Ancient Egyptians believed in an afterlife in which they would enjoy life even after death. Because of this belief they made elaborate preparations for their Pharaohs' burials. The rulers and their families were placed in great pyramids and tombs.

Before being buried, King Tut's body was **mummified** to keep it from decaying. Next his body was wrapped in layers of linen strips and put into a coffin. Finally his mummy was placed in a great tomb, surrounded by such objects as clothes, jewelry, and food. Egyptians believed that these objects would be used by the king in the afterlife.

Although King Tut's rule was brief, the discovery of his tomb has made him the most famous Egyptian Pharaoh. Had it not been for the British archaeologist Howard Carter, his tomb and its amazing treasures might have remained undiscovered.

Trained as an artist, Carter became interested in Egyptian artifacts as a young boy. He combined both interests when he first traveled to Egypt in 1891. There he worked as an artist on an archaeological team, at first making copies of ancient drawings, sculptures, and inscriptions. He then became an archaeologist and discovered several ancient Egyptian tombs. Later he was hired by Lord Carnarvon, a famous collector of Egyptian artifacts, to supervise excavations for him. Carter's goal was to find the tomb of Tutankhamen, which he believed was in the Valley of the Kings.

British archaeologist Howard Carter emerges from the entrance to Tutankhamen's tomb holding a box of artifacts.

Although he didn't have the technology that archaeologists use today, Carter did know that others had found clues that the tomb was in the valley, an ancient burial site. These clues included a cup with the name "Tut-ankh-amun" on it. Encouraged, Carter continued to search. Unfortunately his employer, Lord Carnarvon, was becoming impatient. In 1922 he gave Carter enough money to pay for just one more season of excavation.

Carter increased his efforts. On November 4, 1922, he found the top of a staircase leading to the sealed entrance to a tomb. The entire staircase was finally uncovered about three weeks later. It led to a blocked doorway. The block was removed, revealing a sloping corridor filled with rubble that workers removed with picks, hoes, and carts. Carter found that robbers had broken into the tomb at least twice before and then resealed it. Had the thieves looted the Pharaoh's burial chamber, too?

By this time Lord Carnarvon had joined Carter at the tomb site. The passage beyond the first door to the tomb led to a second door. This door too was blocked with a large stone block covered with plaster. Carter made a hole in the second door and finally peered through. "Can you see anything?" Lord Carnarvon asked. "Yes, wonderful things," Carter answered. On the afternoon of November 26, 1922, Carter broke through the second doorway. He had discovered the tomb of Tutankhamen at last.

Treasures of Tutankhamen's Tomb

The first room that Howard Carter and his team entered was the tomb's antechamber, or waiting room. One door in the antechamber led to a small room called the annex, and a second led to the king's burial chamber. A door in the burial chamber led to a room called the treasury.

Although the tomb contained amazing treasures, it was actually very small in comparison to the tombs of other Egyptian rulers. Building a Pharaoh's tomb took a long time. Because King Tut died so young, the work on his intended burial place had barely started. Archaeologists think that the young Pharaoh was buried in a smaller tomb originally built for someone less important. Because space was limited, the things buried with him, including thrones, boats, and jewelry, were crowded into the tomb.

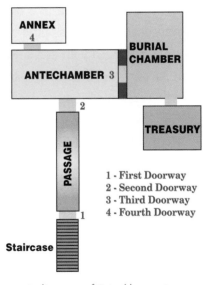

A diagram of Tutankhamen's underground tomb in the Valley of the Kings

In the antechamber, Carter and his team found a jumble of objects, including animal-shaped couches, chariots, and a golden throne. There were two life-sized statues of Tutankhamen, which guarded the entrance to the burial chamber. In keeping with ancient Egyptian beliefs, there were objects that the king would need in the afterlife, such as bows and arrows, farming tools, and food. The team spent several months photographing, clearing, and sorting everything in that one room. In the annex more equipment was found crowded together. About 500 important religious and funeral objects were found in the treasury. The most important was a large, gilded shrine.

The burial chamber contained the most dazzling treasures. This room was decorated with wall paintings of the Pharaoh's funeral and his meeting with the gods after death. When the team first entered the room, they were startled to see one wall that appeared to be made of gold. It was actually a large shrine, made of gilded wood. Inside it were three other gilded shrines. The shrines enclosed a **sarcophagus** carved out of very hard sandstone, containing three nested coffins.

The third coffin, made of solid gold, held the Pharaoh's mummy. The mummy was covered with about 100 items, including jewels and a dagger. Perhaps the most amazing find of all was the solid gold mask that covered the mummy's face. The mummy, which was in poor condition, was studied and returned to its tomb, where it still remains.

Howard Carter spent about ten years uncovering and analyzing the thousands of treasures from the tomb. He and his team recorded and preserved their discoveries so the objects could survive. Today the treasures are on display in the Egyptian Museum in Cairo, Egypt. Visitors from all over the world go there to see the jewelry, chariots, and, of course, the famous golden mask. In the same room as the mask are two of the three coffins from the burial chamber.

Remember that King Tutankhamen wasn't considered to be an important Pharaoh. Yet his tomb contained amazing artifacts made from solid gold. Because of the efforts of Howard Carter and his team, we now know a great deal about the life and death of this young ruler. Carter helped uncover important treasures from a past world that might have been lost to us forever.

This gold innermost coffin from King Tut's tomb is on display at the Egyptian Museum in Cairo, Egypt. The coffin, more than six feet long, was so heavy that it took eight men to lift it.

Crow Canyon Archaeological Center

Archaeologists have been searching for clues about ancient cultures all over the world. In the United States important research has been carried out by the Crow Canyon Archaeological Center. The center has investigated about two dozen sites once inhabited by **ancestral Puebloans** in the Mesa Verde region of southwestern Colorado.

The center's archaeologists study these ancient sites and publish reports. Later the artifacts they discover and their notes are sent to the Anasazi Heritage Center. This is an archaeological museum operated by the U.S. government. In this museum you can see exhibits about the native cultures of the Four Corners region. That is the area in the Southwest where the boundaries of four states meet—Colorado, New Mexico, Arizona, and Utah.

The Crow Canyon Archaeological Center also provides educational programs so that students can work with experienced archaeologists in the field. In this way students in elementary, middle, and high schools learn about the archaeology of the American Southwest. In addition to taking part in excavations, school groups also find out what happens when artifacts are analyzed in a laboratory. Students not only learn how archaeologists excavate a site but also discover how Native Americans lived hundreds of years ago.

Cliff Palace, one of the largest and most famous of the ancient Anasazi cliff dwellings. It is located in Mesa Verde National Park.

The Anasazi, which means "the Ancient Ones" in Navajo, were mainly a farming people who developed an important culture in the Four Corners region. Anasazi is another name for the ancestral Puebloan people. Their civilization developed over about 1,300 years, beginning about A.D. 1. Then the people stopped roaming from place to place, settled down, built permanent homes, and grew crops. Soon the Anasazi made elaborate twisted baskets and pottery.

From about 1100 to 1300, a group of the Anasazi lived in great connected cliff houses, which they built in sheltered places, or alcoves, in the faces of sandstone cliffs. Just think of them as ancient apartment houses. Possibly because of a long drought or the arrival of other groups in the area, the Anasazi abandoned these spectacular cliff houses by A.D. 1300. The dwellings have been researched by archaeologists, who have studied the artifacts found there.

Archaeologists Study Castle Rock Pueblo

The Anasazi left the Four Corners region more than 700 years ago. Some went south; others, west; some joined other groups. However, they left behind clues about their way of life, which were later found in **pueblos** in the area. Castle Rock Pueblo was a village in southwestern Colorado. The people in this village didn't build their homes in the faces of cliffs. Instead, in the 1200s, they built their village around the base and on the top of the Castle Rock **butte**.

People in this community were very active. They grew corn, squash, and beans and hunted deer and other wild game. They lived in family or clan groups and kept busy with such chores as making clothing, pottery, and tools.

We know a great deal about the lives of the people who lived there because from 1990 to 1994, archaeologists from Crow Canyon Archaeological Center excavated and studied the pueblo. They worked with assistants, including students, to find out more about this village.

Archaeologists hoped to find the answers to several important questions:

- ❖ How big was the community at Castle Rock Pueblo?
- ❖ What was daily life like for the people?
- ❖ When did the people leave Castle Rock Pueblo?
- ❖ Why did they leave?

After asking research questions and making a plan for the excavation, the archaeologists and their helpers began work at the site. Many of their tools were very simple, including buckets, whisk brooms, and trowels. Paintbrushes were used to gently remove loose dirt from artifacts without scratching them. Also, wire mesh screens helped workers to find all the artifacts in the dirt they removed. They made maps that recorded exactly what they found.

The team dug in small, square pits during the first two years of excavation. These test pits were like windows into the ground that helped the team look back into history.

Kristin Kuckelman *(top left)*, Senior Research Archaeologist at Crow Canyon Archaeological Center, supervising middle school students at Castle Rock Pueblo

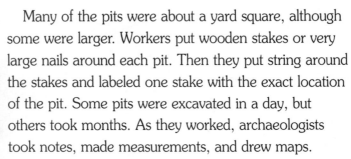

Many of the pits were about a yard square, although some were larger. Workers put wooden stakes or very large nails around each pit. Then they put string around the stakes and labeled one stake with the exact location of the pit. Some pits were excavated in a day, but others took months. As they worked, archaeologists took notes, made measurements, and drew maps.

In time they excavated a whole **kiva** and several rooms. A kiva was usually built below ground and was used for ceremonies and other activities. After uncovering the kiva, archaeologists compared it to buildings at other sites nearby.

While they worked, the team collected samples from burned and unburned wood. Then they used a method called **tree-ring dating** to figure out how old the wood was. It involves counting the yearly growth rings on wooden beams used to make ancient buildings. By comparing the pattern of the tree rings in the beams with a reference sample whose dates they knew, they could tell when the buildings were constructed. Using tree-ring dating, archaeologists believe that Castle Rock Pueblo was built between 1256 and 1274.

The most advanced equipment used at the Castle Rock site was a surveying instrument called a laser transit. This is a very accurate computer on a tripod that was used to map the entire site.

Of course, the archaeologists at the site had a big advantage over Howard Carter, who had worked so long at King Tut's tomb. The team at Castle Rock Pueblo used computers to record their findings and create a database containing the information. After the

Students working in a lab at Crow Canyon

team had finished the excavation, this information was used in writing a final report. Kristin Kuckelman, Senior Research Archaeologist at Crow Canyon, was the primary author. The report took five years to complete and was published on the Internet in 2000.

During the excavation the artifacts from the site were taken to a laboratory for further study. There they were washed, sorted, cataloged, and analyzed. Toothbrushes were used to get the dirt off! However, high-tech equipment was also important. Digital scales were used to weigh the artifacts, and high-powered binocular microscopes were used to examine animal bones and plant remains. Computer data from the laser transit were downloaded into a special program to create maps of the site. Information was always carefully recorded and lab forms were completed.

In many ways the archaeologists at the center followed the same careful methods that Howard Carter did in excavating King Tut's tomb. However, they were able to do their work more quickly because of the computers and other equipment that is now available.

Do you remember the four key questions listed on page 14 that the archaeologists hoped to answer by excavating Castle Rock Pueblo? After completing their work, they had found answers.

◈ Excavations and maps showed that the community contained at least 40 rooms, 15 kivas, 9 towers, and 2 dams. Between 75 and 100 people lived there.

◈ The archaeologists found artifacts showing that the villagers had contact with people who lived beyond the Four Corners region. These goods included pottery made by people who lived in what are now Arizona and New Mexico. In addition, marine shells, used as jewelry, came from the California coast.

◈ Evidence found at the site shows that the people left after 1274. After examining human bones found at Castle Rock Pueblo, archaeologists concluded that some of the villagers died violently. These deaths were likely the result of a conflict, probably an enemy attack. Archaeologists found few artifacts on the floors of the buildings, which raises another question: Did the villagers move their possessions before or after the struggle?

The excavation at Castle Rock Pueblo is over, and important information about the community and its people was learned from the work there. Yet, if you visited the site today, you wouldn't know that the area had ever been disturbed.

Archaeologists have refilled the test pits and buildings with dirt. This ancient pueblo is once again a part of the Southwest landscape, but it isn't forgotten. Visitors who come to Castle Rock Pueblo learn about the culture that existed here hundreds of years ago. More importantly, they also learn to respect the way of life of the Anasazi.

Castle Rock Pueblo excavation site

Machu Picchu: Lost City of the Inca Empire

While the Anasazi were building cliff houses, a great civilization was developing in South America. Around A.D. 1200 the **Incas** were living in what is now the Cuzco area in Peru. By 1438 the Inca empire began to expand, extending more than 2,500 miles along the western coast of South America. In 1532, Spanish explorers captured the Inca emperor and eventually conquered the Incas.

Although the Inca empire was highly developed, there was no writing system. It wasn't until the Spanish conquest that anything was written about this civilization. As a result much of our information has come from archaeological discoveries.

We do know that the Incas were great builders. They constructed an irrigation system in the coastal desert. They cut terraces into the mountainsides so they could grow crops. The Incas also built a network of roads, connecting the empire. We also know that the Incas, like the ancient Egyptians, believed in an afterlife. They made mummies of the dead and believed that these mummies were sacred.

Archaeologists wanted to know more about the Incas. They especially wanted to find Vilcabamba, the lost city from which Inca rulers led a revolt against Spanish rule in the 16th century. Instead of this city an American archaeologist found another site—Machu Picchu.

Archaeologist Hiram Bingham, explored South America in 1906 and 1908. In 1911 he returned to lead a Yale University archaeological expedition. His goal was to find Vilcabamba, in the Andes Mountains. Bingham knew the search would be difficult. Even the Spanish conquerors had never found the city. However, Bingham refused to give up.

After arriving in Cuzco, the ancient Inca capital, Bingham began his search. A farmer who lived near Machu Picchu told him about some ancient ruins and led him to the site. Bingham believed it was the lost city of Vilcabamba.

The next year he returned to Peru and began to excavate the site. His team cleared the area, photographed the site, and made a map of the ruins. He found that terraces built by the Incas more than 500 years ago were still in use! Farmers were still growing their crops there. Later Bingham wrote about his discovery for *National Geographic* magazine.

It wasn't until 1964 that another American archaeologist proved that a different Inca ruin is probably Vilcabamba.

This map shows the location of Machu Picchu in Peru.

The World of Machu Picchu

If Machu Picchu wasn't the city Bingham had hoped to find, what exactly was it? The ruins, located in the Andes Mountains about 50 miles northwest of Cuzco, were surrounded by green hills and snow-covered mountain peaks. The site included hundreds of terraces, many small stone houses, palaces, towers, fountains, and several temples. Archaeologists believe that Machu Picchu was built by the Inca emperor Pachacuti, who ruled from about 1438 to 1471. The real question is why it was built.

Remember that archaeologists are detectives who try to solve mysteries about the past. Their research suggests many ideas to explain what Machu Picchu was used for. Many believe that the site was a royal estate where the emperor could live with his family and servants. Here he could take part in religious activities away from the capital. Other researchers believe that the area could have been used as a fortress or even as an agricultural center.

Archaeologists believe that about 1,000 people lived year-round at Machu Picchu, taking care of the temples and farming on the terraces. They continued to live there until the early- or mid-16th century. No one is sure why they left. Maybe it was a lack of water. Or perhaps people left the area some time after the Spanish conquest began in 1532.

The Temple of the Sun *(inset)* at Machu Picchu

When Hiram Bingham first saw Machu Picchu, he was amazed to find more than 100 stairways cut into the rock, ranging from a few steps to more than 150. Part of the city was divided into compounds, each of which contained six to ten houses where the citizens lived. Each compound had an entrance that could be barred for protection.

On the day he discovered the site, Bingham admired a circular building called the Temple of the Sun. This monument has some of the most beautiful stonework at the site. The walls of the stone tower have small hollowed-out areas where people could leave offerings to the gods. Archaeologists believe that this temple was used to observe the stars and mark the movements of the sun.

West of the main plaza is a monument called the Sacred Stone, which was used for religious activities. This large piece of granite juts out of the earth and faces east and west.

One area of Machu Picchu, called the agricultural section, contained terraces used to grow crops. As a result the city could produce enough food to feed the people who lived there.

The temple district is located in the western part of Machu Picchu. There Bingham found a building called the Principal Temple that had three walls and a foundation of huge rocks. Beyond the temple is an important structure called the Intihuatana ("Hitching Post of the Sun"). Archaeologists believe that this carved, ceremonial sundial was used to mark the movements of the sun and keep track of the changing seasons. It stands six feet tall. The Spanish conquerors had destroyed many similar stone sundials in other cities when they conquered the Incas. The survival of this one proved to Hiram Bingham that the Spanish had never seen Machu Picchu.

The archaeological team that excavated and studied the site wanted to find out more about the daily lives of the people who lived there. In addition to uncovering buildings, monuments, and fountains throughout the city, they also found jugs and food dishes in the southern and eastern sections. These artifacts showed that citizens had lived in these parts of the city. Like archaeologists in ancient Egypt and at Castle Rock Pueblo, Hiram Bingham had used clues found in the present to unlock an ancient mystery about life in a lost city.

Traveling Through Time

The excavations at King Tut's tomb, Castle Rock Pueblo, and Machu Picchu are just three examples of archaeological research taking place all over the world. By studying such sites, archaeologists have been able to make ancient cultures more exciting and real to us. We now have a good idea how ancient Egyptians, the ancestral Puebloans, and the Incas lived their daily lives. In some cases our knowledge of these ancient cultures has been greatly increased by archaeologists' use of modern technology, such as computers and specialized lab equipment, as well as simple tools such as trowels and picks.

Learning about these ancient civilizations has taught us to respect and appreciate their achievements. Understanding our past gives us a feeling of pride in what our ancestors created, but the past belongs to all of us. Archaeologists have made the achievements of various civilizations known to people all over the world.

The work of archaeologists never ends. There are still many sites to be explored on every continent. Someday archaeologists of the future will be studying our culture, too.

Students excavating a pit at Castle Rock Pueblo